Utter Garbage

A Play for Children

Les Ellison

A SAMUEL FRENCH ACTING EDITION

SAMUELFRENCH-LONDON.CO.UK
SAMUELFRENCH.COM

CHARACTERS

Dumpster, an idealistic young garbage rat
Binlid, Dumpster's more conventional uncle
The Lord Vermin, tyrannical ruler of the garbage
Trash, Vermin's snivelling valet
Guard 1 ⎫ Vermin's soldiers (*non speaking*)
Guard 2 ⎭
Captain Horatio Rodent, a sea-faring rat
Mr Hardy Bilge, first mate to Captain Rodent
Sea-Rat 1 ⎫
Sea-Rat 2 ⎬ the crew (*non speaking*)
Sea-Rat 3 ⎭
Hamilton, a well-fed hamster

PRODUCTION NOTE

Most of the action takes place in the rubbish dump where Dumpster lives. A feature of the scene is a drain spout through which Dumpster appears and disappears on his way to and from the roof of a house next to the dump. There is also a vertical grid big enough to allow the rats aboard the sardine can ship to pass through, into the garden scene.

The grid is set in a movable screen to one side of the dump scene. This screen is moved around like a large door as the sardine can passes through the grid (like a large cat flap). When turned around this screen closes off the dump scene and reveals the garden scene where Hamilton lives.

The action at the end of the first act takes place in the audience and requires the effect of car headlights sweeping the auditorium. This can be achieved by inserting a mask, with two circular holes cut in it, between the lamp and lens of a follow-spot.

The animated "cat" is made from various pieces of refuse mounted on poles (representing matches or cocktail sticks) to form the features of a cat's face. The eyes can be bottle tops or bin-lids, the nose a cork, the ears bits of cardboard and the mouth broken combs with a few teeth missing. A little imagination will go a long way here.

Les Ellison

Thank you to
Ian and Cassandra Bullock, Ian and Philippa Hogg
and the Dramarama Theatre Company, Muscat,
Sultanate of Oman

ACT I

A rubbish dump

In a sardine can on the heap of garbage, Binlid lies sleeping

Music. An alarm clock sounds

Binlid sits up, blissfully ignorant of the audience, and sleepily looks around. Eventually he unearths the still ringing alarm clock. He tries to turn it off, growing more and more impatient as his efforts fail. Finally he hurls it off stage. There is the sound of a breaking clock and the release of its main-spring, off. Showing his relief that the ringing has stopped, Binlid climbs out of the can. He is wearing a tattered dressing-gown over his equally tattered clothes. He attempts one or two half-hearted exercises but gives up. From the garbage he pulls a large plate and cleans it by spitting on it and rubbing it with his tail. Rummaging in the garbage he selects a few decomposing and clearly smelly morsels which will constitute his breakfast. Just as he is settling down to eat, he notices the audience. Abandoning his breakfast he moves DS and peers at them curiously. He waves at them. They wave back (hopefully) and he is visibly surprised. He tries waving with both hands and is encouraged by their response. Starting to enjoy this he shouts a greeting: "Hallo", and the audience reply. With more confidence he tries something more involved: "One, two, three". The audience should (with luck) answer, "Four, five, six"

Binlid 'Ere, you're people aren't you? Yeah, I thought so. I knew you weren't rats. I knew that 'cos you 'aven't got tails, see. And you can count. Clever that. Rats can't count. Least not as far as six anyway ... er .... (*He is running out of conversation*) So ... Welcome to the dump. If you don't mind I'm just going to 'ave my breakfast. I'd ask you to join me, but seein' as it's mostly stuff as you lot 'ave chucked out already I can't see you waitin' to eat it now. (*He returns to his breakfast, sitting in front of the drain spout*)

There is the sound of someone shouting as they come shooting down the drain

Dumpster (*off; screaming*) Ahhhhh!

Dumpster hurtles out of the drain spout and lands on top of Binlid

They struggle and eventually disentangle themselves

Binlid Great rats'-tails, Dumpster, what are you doin'? You could 'ave killed me.
Dumpster Sorry, Uncle Binlid. I was on the roof. I lost my footing coming down the drain pipe. It's a good job you were there to break my fall. I could have been badly injured.
Binlid Do anything like that to me again and you will be badly injured, I can promise you that.
Dumpster Sorry.
Binlid What are you doin' on the roof anyway? You know *he* doesn't like·us to go up there. You're going to get yourself in serious trouble if you don't watch it.
Dumpster I know, but you can see so much from the roof. You should come and see. Come on, Uncle Binlid, come and see ...

Dumpster drags Binlid toward the drain spout to the roof

It doesn't take a minute to climb up the drain and you can see for ever; all the way to the edge of the world and ——
Binlid No thanks. I want to keep my paws firmly on the ground and so do you. This is our world; down here in the garbage. It won't do none of us any good you gettin' ideas above your station.

Dumpster looks a little dejected. Binlid mellows

I just don't want you gettin' into any trouble that's all. Hey, if you want to see somethin' different, come and look at this ...

Binlid leads Dumpster DS *to look at the audience*

There. What d'you think?
Dumpster What are they?
Binlid People.
Dumpster People?
Binlid Yeah.
Dumpster Then why aren't they standing on their chairs and going "Aah! Aah!"? Isn't that what people are supposed to do when they see rats?
Binlid I think these are only child-people. You know, like they 'aven't growed up yet. 'Aven't been properly showed what to do. 'Ere watch this.

Binlid shouts "Hallo" and waves at the audience. The audience response frightens Dumpster who screams and hides behind Binlid

It's all right, it's all right. They don't mean any 'arm. 'Ere you 'ave a go. Go on.

Dumpster is reluctant and has to be encouraged by Binlid. Dumpster gives an almost imperceptible wave and a very feeble "Hallo". The audience response freezes him to the spot. Slowly he relaxes and warms to them

There. Quite friendly really. 'Ave anuver go.

Dumpster waves and shouts more enthusiastically. The response encourages him and his waves and shouts become more wild. He is jumping around and having a great time! Binlid's look of pleasure turns to worry as he glances uncertainly around him and tries to quieten Dumpster, and if necessary, the audience

All right, Dumpster. I said, all right, Dumpster ... That's enough, Dumpster. Dumpster! That's enough! (*He grabs him and silences him in mid-wave*) Shh. You got to be more careful. You know there's rats round 'ere as don't like people. Even child-people. There'll be real trouble if they find you talkin' to them. Now if I let you go will you behave yourself?

Dumpster nods his agreement

Promise?

Dumpster nods again

All right then.

Dumpster is released

Dumpster I'm sorry, Uncle Binlid. I see lots of people from the roof but I've never been this close to them before. (*Examining them closely*) Not very big are they.

Binlid Like I said, they's only child-people. But I'll tell you something; they's pretty clever for young 'uns. Watch this. (*To the audience*) One ... two ... three ...

The audience responds "Four, five, six" as before. Dumpster is awestruck

Dumpster They can count.

Binlid Told you they were clever.

Dumpster All the way to six. I wish I could count to six.

Binlid Countin's a people thing. It's not for us rats to be doin' things like countin'. Now come on, this place is far too tidy and it must be nearly ten o'clock. He'll be here any minute now.

Binlid takes off his dressing-gown and sets about scattering one or two bags of rubbish from the garbage

Dumpster Why doesn't he like it tidy? Why does it always have to be a mess? And why don't we have any flowers? From the roof I can see lots of flowers; red ones and yellow ones all in pretty patterns and ——

Binlid For the last time, Dumpster, I don't want to hear any more about what you can see from the roof! Now get on wiv your garbage.

Trash enters at the back of the auditorium, flanked by two Guards, carrying spears. He plays a flat-toned fanfare on a battered brass instrument. The fanfare falters and fails into a fit of coughing and spitting

Trash Me lords, lady rats, assorted rodents, other species of small furry animals and anybody else who doesn't want a bite guaranteed to give 'em tetanus, had better stand up to greet His Ratship. You will salute His Ratship in the traditional manner by doing this ... (*he puts his hands to his head like ears*) and going "Eek, eek". Got that? Good. (*He coughs and clears his throat in a most disgusting manner then stands to attention and announces*) His Ignoble Ratship The Lord Vermin. Ruler of Refuse, Defender of the Dump and Guardian of the Garbage.

Vermin enters and is lead to the stage by Trash

The Guards prod the audience with their spears to make them stand for Vermin. Binlid and Dumpster prepare to receive the party

Binlid Mornin' Your Ratship, sir. Welcome to our stinking heap of garbage. So mean of you to blight us with your presence.

Trash Cut the pleasantries, Binlid. You know His Ratship comes every day at this time to check on the state of his refuse.

Vermin And as for stinking heap of garbage I find this pile of refuse almost pleasant. Very disappointing.

Dumpster kicks aimlessly in the rubbish and finds an aerosol air-freshener. He picks it up and reads the label

How many flies have you got here?

Binlid (*shrugging*) You know I can't count.

Dumpster shakes the aerosol and prepares to use it. He starts to spray it into the air during the following

Vermin You shouldn't be able to count them even if you could count them! There should be a million. This garbage just isn't smelly enough. And why is there no rotting fruit? Where's the squashy tomatoes? Where's the potato peelings? There's not nearly enough waste paper. In fact, the whole place is just too tidy. Too tidy ...

Vermin sniffs the air and notices Dumpster

What in rats'-tails ... Guards. Guards arrest that rat!

The Guards grab Dumpster and bring him to Vermin

What is that?

Trash (*taking the aerosol and reading the label*) It's ... er, "Fragrant Flowers", the freshener that eliminates unpleasant smells and brings the scent of a thousand country flowers to your kitchen ... Oh, and it's ozone friendly.

Vermin (*snatching the aerosol from Trash*) I know what it is. What's it doing in the paws of a garbage rat!

Binlid (*in Dumpster's defence*) He means no harm, Your Ratship, sir. He's only playin'. Found it in the garbage didn't you, Dumpster. Just wanted to know how it works. You know what it's like when you're a young rat. He's only a nipper.

Trash Oh, very good. Yes. Nipper rat, rat nipper. Very funny.

Vermin Trash?

Trash Yes, Your Ratship?

Vermin Do shut up or I'll have the guards run you through with a spear. All right?

Trash (*recovering his composure*) Anything you say, Your Ratship. (*He gives one more stifled giggle*)

Vermin (*reading the aerosol*) Thousand flowers indeed.

Dumpster Well it's better than a thousand flies.

Vermin What?

Dumpster That's all we ever get here. Flies. Flies and rubbish. And more flies and more rubbish. We never get any flowers. Why don't we ever get any flowers? (*He pulls away from the guards and advances on Vermin*) You're the Governor of Garbage why don't we ever get any flowers?

Binlid gets between Dumpster and Vermin

Binlid Don't pay any attention to him, Your Ratship. It's the sun. It sometimes affects him like this, but he'll be all right in a minute (*to Dumpster*) won't you!

Dumpster sulks off and kicks about in the rubbish. During the following, he finds a brush and begins to sweep up

Vermin As I was saying, I find the garbage here most disappointing. I see no rusted tins, no dangerous broken glass and worst of all no putrefying vegetables. How do you hope to have a decent stink when there are no putrefying vegetables? (*He catches sight of Dumpster*) What in rats'-tails is that animal doing now? Guards!

The Guards grab Dumpster again

Dumpster I was just tidying up a bit. It's a bit of a mess over there and it all gets really smelly if it's left lying around in the sun. Then we get all these flies and ——

Vermin (*losing his temper*) This is a rubbish dump. It is supposed to be a mess, it is supposed to smell. It is supposed to have flies. Why? Because it is garbage, and we are rats: you are a rat, I am a rat. We live in garbage, we thrive in garbage and I am the Governor of Garbage and I like it this way!

Dumpster I just thought if I brushed up a little then ——

Vermin Don't think. Thinking is dangerous. Leave thinking to those who can handle it. You can get into a lot of trouble through thinking, can't you, Trash.

Trash Yes. Yes, you can … I think?

Vermin Fresh air, flowers. Where does a young rat get such dangerous ideas, I wonder? (*He looks accusingly at Binlid*)

Binlid No idea, Your Ratship. Er … no idea at all.

Dumpster From the roof.

Vermin From the what?

Dumpster is about to answer but Binlid grabs him across the mouth

Binlid From the woof, er ... Your Ratship, sir. From the woof! Woof! Only yesterday we were talking about how wonderful it is to live in garbage when stone me if this dog doesn't come along and start going on about flowers and stuff. Fair terrified young Dumpster I can tell you.

Vermin (*suspiciously*) From the dog, then?

Binlid Woof woof.

Vermin Not from the roof?

Binlid Oh, no.

Vermin Good. Because the punishment for rats found on the roof is very severe. (*To Dumpster*) Very severe indeed.

Vermin catches sight of the audience

Aagh! Guards! Guards! Out there. Look, people. Horrid people. See them? Hundreds of them.

The Guards take up a defensive position in front of Vermin

Binlid They're only child-people, Your Ratship.

Vermin Only child-people? Only child-people?

Binlid Yeah, nothin' to be afraid of. 'Aven't growed up properly yet. Quite small really, not dangerous at all.

Vermin Child-people are the most dangerous of all because they haven't grown up yet. Because they're still learning, still thinking. Once they've grown up they stop that nonsense. Then they're safe. Harmless, even. But not these, you can see it in their eyes. Worse than cats.

Dumpster They can count too. Watch: (*to the audience*) one ... two ... three ...

The audience reply is a horror to Vermin and Trash

Vermin Aagh! Counting. See I told you they were dangerous.

Dumpster They're only numbers.

Vermin They start with only numbers but then comes letters and alphabets. Soon it's reading and learning. Then before you know where you are they start thinking and have ... *ideas*.

Dumpster But what's wrong with having ——

Vermin Because after ideas come questions. (*He takes a spear from one of the Guards and prods Dumpster*) And some questions deserve very, very, very, sharp answers indeed. And that is a dangerous thing for those who ask too many questions. If you get the point.

Trash Oh, very good. Yes. Sharp point, point sharp. Very funny.

Trash's amusement is cut off by a razor-edged look from Vermin

Vermin I hold you responsible for this, Binlid. You're his guardian, he's your nephew, it's up to you to teach him what it means to be a rat.

In his next speech Vermin walks about the dump giving his instructions. He is still waving the spear around and unwittingly knocks Trash into a heap of rubbish

I want this place messed up properly. I want it so smelly I can't breathe. I want so many flies buzzing around I can't hear myself think. I want rusty tins, I want broken glass, I want waste paper, rotting fruit and putrefying vegetables. And I want it all disgustingly messy!

Trash emerges from the rubbish where he fell, covered in refuse, very dirty and clearly very, very smelly

Trash. You dirty rat.

Trash Oh, thank you. Thank you, Your Ratship. Thank you. That's the nicest thing anyone has ever said to me.

Vermin And I want it all done today. I will be back. (*He makes to leave*) And when I come back, if I don't like what I see, you and your nephew will be cat food! And get these child-people out of here. Worse than cats. They make me nervous.

Vermin, Trash and the Guards leave

Dumpster Oh, Uncle, why does he have to be so horrid? And why do we have to live in this filthy dump ...? (*He impersonates Vermin*) I want this place messed up properly. I want it so smelly I can't breathe. I want so many flies buzzing around I can't hear myself think. Well I don't! (*As if shouting after Vermin*) I hate it here. I want to live in a place that's got flowers and doesn't smell of rotten vegetables!

Binlid Steady on, Dumpster. You heard what he said and he wasn't jokin'. Look, it ain't perfect here, I know that. But we just got to make the best we can, that's all. Come on, give us a hand. We can have this place really disgustin' in no time.

Dumpster (*sulking*) Shan't.

Binlid Oh, come on.

Dumpster No. (*He looks at the audience*) It's not fair. I bet child-people don't live in rubbish.

Binlid Oh, I don't know. I got into a child-people's bedroom once. Looked much the same as this really.

Dumpster Then why's Vermin so frightened of them, the child-people?

Binlid See, there you go again: more questions. If your father was alive ——

Dumpster But he isn't is he?

Binlid No, but ——

Dumpster And my mother's not either is she?

Binlid No ——

Dumpster A cat ate them didn't it? A cat ate them.

Binlid (*running out of patience*) Yes! A cat ate them!

Dumpster Then why is Vermin more frightened of child-people than cats? Child-people don't eat us and we can give them very nasty bites if they get too close, can't we?

Binlid I've 'ad just about enough of this, I'm off. I missed my breakfast 'cos of you. (*Putting on a scruffy coat and scarf*) I'm goin' down the town, there's always a few chicken bones and 'arf-eaten sandwiches lyin' around down there. You stay 'ere an' do what you want. I'm finished with you. You're on your own.

Binlid storms off

Dumpster takes his frustration out on the rubbish then sits and sulks. Suddenly he has an idea. He makes his way to the drain spout and, making sure no-one is watching, he climbs into the spout and disappears

Music: the theme from Captain Pugwash

Captain Rodent (*off*) Stroke. Stroke. Stroke ...

Captain Rodent enters through the grid calling through a megaphone. He is sitting in a ship's life-belt on a small trolley pulled by a bedraggled Bilge and the three equally bedraggled Sea-Rats. There is a telescope on the trolley

Hard at starboard ... Steady as she goes ... (*He ad libs as necessary as they move across the stage*) Half ahead both, prepare to drop anchor. Finished with engines, Mr Bilge.

Bilge Engines stopped, Captain Rodent sir.

Captain Rodent Drop anchor, Mr Bilge.

Bilge Ay, ay, sir.

The Sea-Rats help Captain Rodent up from the trolley and pull the life-belt ashore. Bilge lines up the Sea-Rats for inspection

Ship's company ... 'tenshun! Ship's company ready for inspection, sir.

Captain Rodent Very good, Mr Bilge. (*He inspects them*). Fine body of rats, Mr Bilge. Proud to share a ship with all of them. Only wish I had a ship to share.

Bilge Not to worry, sir. An accident like that could happen to anybody.

Captain Rodent What, sunk in mid-ocean by a direct hit from a flying alarm clock? Don't think so, Mr Bilge. And neither will a court martial. Looks rather more like negligence than accident.

Bilge Worse things happen at sea, sir.

Captain Rodent It did happen at sea, Mr Bilge, or were you asleep between decks as well?

Bilge At least there was no loss of life.

Captain Rodent Good man, Mr Bilge. Always the loyal first mate.

Bilge Thank you, sir. (*He salutes*) Permission to dismiss the rats.

Captain Rodent As you wish. Give them twenty-four hours' shore leave, all of them. I don't think we'll be needing anyone to stay and look after the ship tonight.

Bilge Very good, sir.

Bilge dismisses the Sea-Rats who forage a little in the rubbish then sit as a group eating what they've managed to find. Captain Rodent wanders DS and surveys the audience through the wrong end of his telescope

Captain Rodent So Mr Bilge, what port is this?

Bilge Not entirely sure, sir. 'Fraid we're sailing what you might call uncharted waters.

Captain Rodent Sailed off the edge of the map, eh?

Bilge It's more a case of the map that sailed off, sir. Charts, ship's log, everything. The only thing we managed to save was a ship's life-belt.

Captain Rodent Well I can't make out any landmarks from here. Everything seems so far away.

Bilge With your permission, sir ...

Bilge takes the telescope from Captain Rodent and offers it back the right way around

Captain Rodent Oh. That's much better. (*Suddenly astounded*) Well sew five arms on my jacket and call me an octopus! There's rats out there with no tails on.

Bilge Six, sir.

Captain Rodent Sorry?

Bilge Six more arms. Octopus have eight arms all together, sir.

Captain Rodent Counting? Well that's jolly clever Mr Bilge, but they've still got no tails. Even a thickee rat can count to erm … one?

Bilge Actually they're people, sir. Child-people to be exact.

Captain Rodent Not erm … not rats then.

Bilge No, sir.

Captain Rodent Well they've still got no tails.

Bilge Correct, sir.

Captain Rodent Thought so. Got to have the eyes of a hawk to be a great sea captain. Sharp eyes, sharp ears and lightning reflexes. Always alert to the possibility of danger …

Captain Rodent turns to walk away and trips over the life-belt, falling into a heap of rubbish and losing his hat. He recovers quickly, leaping to his feet and putting his hat on back to front

There you see that. See how I dived out of danger and recovered with not a whisker out of place? You've got to see danger coming and learn to avoid it to be a sea captain.

Bilge Danger such as flying alarm clocks?

Captain Rodent Ah … Yes. Well it won't happen again I can promise you that. Always on the lookout for danger from any quarter. Leave no place unguarded. Never taken by surprise. Well, not twice anyway. (*He moves to stand in front of the drain spout*) No, Mr Bilge. You have to get up very early in the morning to catch Captain Rodent out twice in the same day.

We hear Dumpster screaming as he comes shooting down the tube

Dumpster (*off*) Ahhhhh!

Dumpster hurtles out of the drain spout and lands on top of Captain Rodent

They struggle to disentangle themselves. Bilge is unmoved

Bilge And what time did you get up this morning, young rat?

Captain Rodent I say, young fellow, dashed near scuppered me good and proper there.

Dumpster Sorry. What are you doing here?

Captain Rodent Ah. Introductions, jolly good. Mr Bilge, fall the rats in.

Bilge lines up the Sea-Rats; they salute as they are named

Captain Horatio Rodent, First Mate Mr Hardy Bilge and the ship's company of the Good Ship *Wastage*; finest cardboard box on the high sea … or rather under it.

Dumpster Oh. Pleased to meet you all.

Captain Rodent And you are?

Dumpster Dumpster. I er … live here.

A nod from Bilge dismisses the Sea-Rats

Captain Rodent Up the drain spout. Dashed strange house for a rat. Bit damp I shouldn't wonder.

Dumpster No, I only fell down the drain. I live in the garbage with my Uncle Binlid. But I like to go up on the roof — you won't tell will you?

Captain Rodent Oh. Mum's the word.

Bilge But why the roof?

Dumpster To get away from all this. From the roof you can see so much more: gardens and flowers and trees and … and … But all you can see from down here is rubbish.

Captain Rodent I thought you land-type rats liked all this garbage and stuff.

Dumpster Not this one. I hate garbage. I hate the sight of it. I hate the smell. I hate the flies. I hate it! Hate it! Hate it …

Captain Rodent Steady on …

Dumpster attacks the rubbish with such venom that the Sea-Rats, who were enjoying a peaceful snack, are thrown into confusion and finish up in a heap on the floor. He is eventually restrained and consoled a little by Bilge

Bilge Easy does it, young fella-me-rat. This isn't going to get us anywhere now, is it … Hmm?

Dumpster (*reluctantly*) No.

Bilge (*encouragingly*) Come on, chin up. Shoulders back. That's better. Now we can try and do something about it, yes?

Bilge gives a very clear wink to Captain Rodent who shows surprise and looks behind to see who Bilge is winking at

I said: now we can do something about it. Yes?

It suddenly dawns on Captain Rodent that Bilge is talking to him

Captain Rodent Ah. Yes … er. Well forgive me if I'm wrong, but I can't help getting the feeling that you're not entirely happy here. Get the impression you'd like to ... leave.

He has Dumpster's undivided attention and Bilge's approval

Like to get away from this place altogether. Like to see a bit of the world, perhaps. Sail the sewers; that vast underground waterway that links everywhere to ... well, everywhere else, really. Maybe have a bit of an adventure, even.

Dumpster Oh, yes. Yes please!

Captain Rodent Well, there's always room in any ship of mine for a likely young rat sound in wind and limb and with a taste for adventure. Only problem is I haven't any ship.

Bilge Beg pardon, sir. It's not an insoluble problem, the ship. It's just a case of finding a vessel that displaces more than its own weight of water. Archimedes' Principle.

Captain Rodent Science. I love it. Have the rats scout around a bit maybe they can find a couple of these ... principle things.

The Sea-Rats rummage around in the garbage and drag out the sardine can that Binlid had been sleeping in, his blanket and a few sticks. They assemble these on the trolley into a boat with a short mast and the blanket as a sail, then stand to attention

Jolly good show. This Archimedes chap must have been pretty keen on sardines. Always preferred kippers myself ...

Bilge (*politely impatient*) Sir ...

Captain Rodent Oh, right. Well, better get on with the launching then — got to give the old tub a name. Dumpster, any ideas?

Dumpster I want to call it ... the *New World*.

Captain Rodent Very well. I name this tin er ... ship: the *New World*. Pity, rather fancied the *Saucy Sue* myself. Oh, well. Right, everybody on board. Come on, pip-pip. Dumpster to the err ... sharp end sort of thing. Myself a mid-ships and the jolly Sea-Rats in the er ..., in the ...

Bilge (*running out of patience*) Stern, sir. Stern!

Capt Rodent Well I rather saw myself as an amiable sort of chap. But if that's what it takes, Mr Bilge ... (*Sternly*) Cast off fore and aft, half ahead and steady as she goes.

Music: the theme from Captain Pugwash

When they are all in position the sardine can is propelled around the stage by the Sea-Rats with Captain Rodent ad libbing commands as necessary. Dumpster has the telescope and is keeping look-out. Bilge is not in the sardine can — he opens the grid, changing the scene to Hamilton's garden as the sardine can passes through

On the command, ship's company will salute the child-people and child-people will do us the compliment of returning the salute. Ship's company … salute.

They all salute and the sardine can is moved toward the grid

Set course for the sewers, Mr Bilge. Off we go. To find the New World. To boldly go where no rat has gone before.
Bilge Oh, well said, sir.
Captain Rodent Yes. Thank you, Mr Bilge.

The sardine can and all its crew pass into the grid. The grid is opened and the scene moved around by Bilge so that they immediately pass out of the grid and into the garden scene. There is grass and flowers and so on. It is as bright and clean as the dump was dull and dirty

Dumpster (*looking through the telescope; excitedly*) Land, land. I can see land.
Captain Rodent Land ho, everyone. Prepare to run aground.

Sound effects: the ship running aground. The sardine can beaches on the grass and pitches on to its side. All the crew fall into a heap

Really must find a better way of stopping these things.

Dumpster is first to recover his feet. He wanders around trying to take it all in. To him this is heaven. Captain Rodent dusts himself down. Bilge joins him. The Sea-Rats attend to the sardine can

Still, not bad for a maiden voyage. Not bad at all.
Dumpster Flowers! Look flowers. Real flowers …

Dumpster picks a bunch of the flowers and smells them. This is a wonderful new experience which he wants everyone to share. He thrusts them into the faces of Captain Rodent and Bilge for them to smell too

Look, flowers. Smell them … You smell them.

Dumpster gives the flowers to Captain Rodent and wanders happily away to the opposite side of the stage

I never imagined anything like this. And no rubbish anywhere. No tins, no paper, no rotting fruit. We must have sailed a million miles. We must have sailed past the edge of the world. Or even further.

Bilge I don't think so, young fella-me-rat. By my reckoning we haven't sailed much more than ten, twenty yards. Of course that's the direct route, by the sewers. Be quite a bit further over land what with roads and traffic and all.

Dumpster Then all this is just next door to the rubbish dump?

Bilge More or less. Of course, you couldn't get here without a ship. And a dream.

Dumpster But it's not a dream. It's real, and I'm going to live here for ever and ever and ever and ever and ...

Hamilton enters, wearing a tracksuit. She fails to notice all the others and jogs ds to do a few exercises facing the audience, but she tires quickly. She addresses the audience

Hamilton Hi, kids! I'm just a bit late this morning so I'm trying to catch up on my exercises. That's the trouble with being a hamster, you spend most of your life asleep and it's not good for the old waistline. Of course, there is that wheel thing that goes round and round, but it's good to get a little fresh air now and again. See you later ...

She turns and catches sight of Captain Rodent and his party

Aaah! Rats! Rats, dirty rotten rats. Go on, shoo. Get out of here. Go on the lot of you. Shoo!

Capt Rodent Madam, may I remind you that you're addressing an officer and a gentlerat.

Hamilton I'm addressing a lunatic.

Dumpster (*coming up behind her*) Hallo, my name's Dumpster.

Hamilton Aah! Another one. Go on, shoo.

Dumpster I only said hallo.

Hamilton Oh, yes. It only starts with "hallo". And before you know where you are it's "goodbye". "Nice to have met you, sorry about your nice little garden."

Dumpster (*innocently*) Yes it's a very nice garden, is it yours?

Hamilton It is. And it's going to stay that way. I'm not having it spoilt by bunch of garbage rats.

Hamilton runs Dumpster practically off the stage then turns and catches sight of Captain Rodent's bunch of flowers

Oh, you've started already, have you? Picking the flowers indeed ...

Captain Rodent hides the flowers behind his back. Hamilton attacks him, forcing him and the rest of his crew back into the sardine can

Vandals! That's all you are, vandals. Now get out of my garden. (*Pointing to the sardine can*) And take that filthy rubbish with you. Go on, get out.
Captain Rodent Back to the ship. All hands to battle stations. Full speed astern ...

Captain Rodent and his crew propel the sardine can away from the garden scene bidding farewell to Dumpster as they go

Farewell, young Dumpster. 'Fraid you're on your own now. Good luck.
Bilge Hope you find your New World.

The sardine can and crew disappear off

Hamilton turns on the bewildered Dumpster

Hamilton And you needn't think you're staying either. Go on. Get away with you.
Dumpster But how ...?
Hamilton The same way as you came. Go on. Shoo.
Dumpster I can't. I came with them and they've gone without me.
Hamilton (*sarcastically*) Oh, dear.
Dumpster And anyway, I don't want to.
Hamilton What you want is neither here nor there.
Dumpster I can't leave and I won't. So there. (*He sits down*).
Hamilton Oh, yes you will. You'll get back to the rubbish dump where your sort belong. There's no place here for the likes of you.
Dumpster No. I'm *not* going back. I'm sick of living in the rubbish dump. It's dirty, it's smelly and I hate it. Just because I was born in rubbish doesn't mean I have to spend all my life in it. I want to live where there's flowers and grass and fresh air. I want to live here! I'd rather die than go back there.
Hamilton Ay, and you probably will too.
Dumpster What? (*He stands and approaches Hamilton*)
Hamilton Don't get me wrong, it's nothing to do with me. I'd be glad of the

company. It's them, the people. Once they know there's rats in the garden they'll put down traps and poison and all sorts of things.

Dumpster But why?

Hamilton Because rats are dirty smelly animals. And where you get rats you get rubbish and filth and disease.

Dumpster That's not fair. I'm as clean as you are ——

Hamilton (*catching scent of Dumpster*) That's as maybe.

Dumpster — and it's not rats' rubbish, it's people's rubbish. Rats just live in it, that's all. It's people that make rubbish, dumping it all over the place. Filthy smelly stuff.

Hamilton Well they still won't let you in their garden.

Dumpster They let you. They don't put traps down for you. They don't try and poison you, do they?

Hamilton Certainly not.

Dumpster Why?

Hamilton (*smugly*) Because I'm their pet.

Hamilton heads off DS *and resumes her exercises. She is followed by the inquisitive Dumpster who joins in some of them, puzzled at her behaviour*

Dumpster Pet rat?

Hamilton (*affronted*) Pet hamster.

Dumpster And they let you live in their garden.

Hamilton Well in their house, actually.

Dumpster In their house? And they don't poison you?

Hamilton Oh, no. In fact they feed me rather well.

Dumpster Chicken bones, and potato peelings and things?

Hamilton (*shocked*) Certainly not. Healthy foods. Like sunflower seeds and peanuts and oats. And just occasionally a little fresh fruit.

While Dumpster speaks Hamilton lies on the floor and does a few cycling motions in the air before collapsing, exhausted

Dumpster Fresh fruit. I've never tasted anything that's not squashy or smelly, or squashy and smelly. And I have to dig it out of the rubbish myself. You're really lucky, you are. Beautiful place to live, fresh air and loads of food. I wish I was you ... whoever you are.

Hamilton Sorry, never introduced myself. Name's Hamilton. Give us a hand up, there's a good rat.

Dumpster helps get Hamilton back on her feet

Thanks, rather too many sunflower seeds, I think.

Dumpster How can people be so good to you and so rotten to me? How can they make beautiful gardens like this and make horrible smelly garbage at the same time? (*To the audience*) You wouldn't make so much rubbish if you had to live in it!

Hamilton Keep your whiskers on, Dumpster, it's not their fault.

Dumpster Yes it is, they're people and they make rubbish.

Hamilton They're child-people. And I think you'll find they've got some pretty strong ideas of their own on that subject.

Dumpster looks sceptically at Hamilton

You must have noticed there's actually a lot less rubbish about these days.

Dumpster (*turning on Hamilton*) No I hadn't, actually. But then I don't live in beautiful garden and have all my meals provided for me either.

Hamilton It's not all free food and gardens.

Dumpster No?

Hamilton No. You have to live in a cage for one thing, and there's no privacy. You get woken up by kids who want to play just when you've settled down for a nap. And then there's that awful wheel thing. Round and round and round … You're just not your own animal.

Dumpster At least I can do much as I please. But I'm not allowed to leave the dump.

Hamilton And I'm not allowed to leave the cage.

Dumpster Then what are you doing in the garden.

Hamilton I've escaped. Much like you, I imagine.

Dumpster nods guiltily

I'm running away. No more cages, no more wheels. You can come too if you like.

Dumpster Where to?

Hamilton A better place!

Dumpster A better place.

They stand together heroically

Hamilton With no cages!

Dumpster And no rubbish!

Hamilton And definitely no wheels!

Dumpster How do we get there?

Hamilton We go and search for it.

Dumpster Where?

Hamilton If you had as many answers as you've got questions we'd be there and back by now. Look, it has to be somewhere out there. Now we can go and look for it or we can stay here and get put in a cage or a trap. Are you with me?

Dumpster (*enthusiastically*) Yes!

Hamilton Right. Here's the plan ...

Hamilton paces the stage with a military air and outlines the plan as if it were an escape from a POW camp. Dumpster follows eagerly behind trying to keep in step and nodding or shaking his head as appropriate. At some point they get out of synch and finish up very close and face to face for Dumpster's line

Neither of us can swim, correct? And since your friends have disappeared we don't have a boat either, so we can't escape through the sewers. Flying is out of the question. We could dig a tunnel. But we are rodents not moles. The only viable route therefore is overland — i.e.: through the streets.

Dumpster Isn't that dangerous?

Hamilton Oh dear, I hadn't thought of that. Cars, lorries. Taxis. Skateboards. Yes, I suppose it is.

Dumpster My uncle Binlid told me that if a car or a lorry is heading toward you, the safest place for a small animal is right between the lights. If you can do that the tyres go past on either side ——

Hamilton He's obviously never heard of Reliant Robins.

Dumpster — so all we have to do is keep out of the headlights.

Hamilton Well it's worth a try. Let's go. To a better world!

Dumpster A better world!

They set off across the stage and down into the audience

Music: the theme from The Great Escape. *Suddenly the music is cut dead by the sound of a car speeding in very close and zooming away into the distance. Its headlights sweep them and the audience in two focused spotlight beams*

Hamilton Aaaah!

Dumpster That was a close one. Come on, stay together. And keep out of the lights.

Together they run up and down the aisles while spotlights with accompanying car noises sweep the audience. While attention is focused in the audience the scene is reset to the rubbish dump

Dumpster and Hamilton become separated. They call to each other across the audience to keep out of the lights. Eventually they run back on to the stage from opposite sides and collide, c. As they impact together they are caught in a strong spotlight. At the sound of screeching tyres they look in horror to the audience. There is a huge crash

Black-out

CURTAIN

ACT II

The rubbish dump

All the props necessary to make the cat should be in place. Hamilton is unseen behind some sacks of garbage

Binlid enters with a takeaway bag containing a burger

Binlid Dumpster. Dumpster? 'Ere. Where are you, you rascal. Look, I've brought you a beefburger. It's been run over by a car, but it's not bad. Least, not once you've picked the stones out it isn't ... Dumpster!

He spits on the burger and rubs it on his sleeve to clean it, then resumes his search. He is calling up the drain spout when he hears Hamilton moaning

Hamilton Oh ...
Binlid Dumpster?
Hamilton Oh. Ohhh ...
Binlid Dumpster? Is that you, young rat ... Where are you?
Hamilton Oh ... Oh ... Ohhh ...
Binlid Dumpster!

Binlid drops his goods and rushes into the garbage. He throws aside a few bags of rubbish expecting to find Dumpster and is stopped dead at the sight of the injured Hamilton who, still a little dazed, sits up, becoming visible to the audience

Great rats'-tails! Who are you?
Hamilton Oh oh oh oh ohhh ...
Binlid Well you're in bad shape, whoever you are. Hang on a minute an' I'll get you out of there.

Binlid moves some more rubbish and eases Hamilton to her feet, leading her DS. *Hamilton has obvious bruising to her forehead, left arm and right shin. She is generally dishevelled*

You are in a mess. Sit there while I try and find somethin' to patch you up.

He sits her down again and makes her comfortable before going back to search in the rubbish

I don't know who you are. An' you really shouldn't be 'ere at all ...

He finds some strips of white cloth and a soft-drink can that still has some liquid in it. He brings them to Hamilton and bandages her head and leg and puts her arm in a crude sling

But it wouldn't do to leave you just lyin' there, all bashed up an' such. You look like you've been in a right scrap; even lost most of your tail.

Hamilton This is all the tail I'm supposed to have. I'm a hamster.

Binlid Hamster? Well we don't get many of those round 'ere. Thought you was indoor animals. Oh, my name's Binlid. (*He wipes his paw on his front and shakes hands*) Pleased to meet you.

Hamilton (*trying to get up*) And I'm Hamilton. I was just ...

Binlid Easy now ... (*He sits her down again*) You just sit there and save your strength. Dumpster'll be long in a minute then we'll see if we can't fix you a bit of a ——

Hamilton Dumpster. Did you say Dumpster?

Binlid Yeah. 'E's my nephew. 'Ere, you 'aven't seen him, 'ave you?

Hamilton Well ... I sort of saw him, earlier this afternoon.

Binlid Oh, good. 'Cos I've got 'is supper 'ere. (*He picks up the squashed beefburger*) Where's 'e gone then?

Hamilton I'm afraid "gone" might be the right word.

Binlid What d'you mean? (*Beginning to fear the worst*) Where is 'e, what's 'appened to 'im?

Hamilton We were crossing the road. We tried to keep out of the headlights, like you told him to. But there were so many cars and then ——

Binlid You got my Dumpster run over by a car?

Hamilton I think it was more of a lorry.

Binlid You got my Dumpster flattened out like a ... like a ... (*Upset and enraged, he threatens Hamilton with the squashed beefburger but no words come out*)

Hamilton It's all my fault. And to think I tried to throw him out of the garden, and you've been so good to me here. I'm so sorry, Mr Binlid, really I am ...

Binlid (*still angry*) Yeah, well sorry ain't goin' a bring my Dumpster back is it!

Hamilton I should never have let him come with me. I should have gone to look for a better world by myself. But without his help I wouldn't have even got this far.

Binlid (*after a silence*) A better world you say.
Hamilton Yes. He had this dream ...
Binlid Yeah. I know all about it. (*His anger is gone*) Always was a bit of a dreamer, our Dumpster. Always gettin' ideas. Spent too much time on the roof, that was 'is trouble. I warned 'im something' like this would 'appen if 'e wasn't careful.

Binlid has moved to the drain spout and pats it affectionately as if it was his nephew. Hamilton comes across to console him

Hamilton I really am very sorry.
Binlid It's not your fault. Somethin' like this was bound to happen sooner or later. Just wish I'd 'ad a chance to say goodbye instead of shoutin' at 'im.

Their conversation is cut short by an off-stage fanfare from Trash and the entry of Vermin, Trash and the two Guards

Trash (*to the audience*) Stand and greet His Ignoble Ratship, the Lord Vermin: Ruler of the Refuse, Defender of the Dump, Guardian of the Garbage. Rise and salute His Ratship. (*He leads them in the salute as before*) Be seated.

Vermin looks approvingly at the garbage which Binlid scattered around while getting Hamilton out of the rubbish

Vermin Good work, Binlid. Good work. I'm pleased to see you've made an effort to make the place a little more disgraceful.
Hamilton Disgraceful indeed! The whole place is a disgrace. I'm not surprised Dumpster wanted to leave.
Binlid (*to Hamilton*) Shhh. You'll get us into trouble.
Vermin And who is that creature? (*Suspiciously*) Bit short in the tail, for a rat.

A furious Hamilton is about to show Vermin exactly what sort of creature she is when she is pulled back by Binlid

Binlid This is er ... a cousin of mine. Yeah, she's just passin' through. Aren't you. 'Ad a bit of a brush wiv a cat on the way 'ere. Nothin' too serious, few bruises an' all, but it bit off most of her tail. Didn't it, cousin?
Vermin (*not really satisfied*) And where's that runt of a nephew?
Hamilton Runt, indeed!

Again Hamilton is restrained by Binlid

Binlid He's er ... gone, Your Ratship.
Vermin Gone?
Binlid Yes, Your Ratship.
Vermin (*suspicious that Dumpster is on the roof again*) Where to?
Binlid To ... to ... er ...
Hamilton (*as much to Binlid as Vermin*) To a better place.
Vermin Good. Never liked him anyway. Too many ideas. Now to business.
  Binlid, I have a proposition to make: how would you like to be my number
  two?
Binlid Number two?
Vermin Yes: after one but before three.
Binlid But that's counting.
Vermin Yes.
Binlid But you said ——
Vermin Oh, counting's all right for some rats, rats who can handle it and
  won't cause trouble. Rats like ... you for instance?
Binlid But it's not all right for rats like Dumpster?
Vermin Certainly not. And it's not all right for child-people either.
Binlid So what have you got in mind?
Vermin Expansion, Binlid. Major infestation. More rubbish. More garbage.
  Bigger and bigger dumps and more and more of them.
Binlid So?
Vermin So I've formed the SRS. The Special Rat Service. A team of
  specially trained rats who don't know the meaning of fear. In fact, they
  don't know the meaning of anything.

Vermin leads Binlid DS *to the audience*

A team of rats trained to work alone in parks and gardens all over the city.
Working undercover nibbling through sacks of rubbish. Chewing through
bundles of refuse. Gnawing through bins and boxes. Wherever rubbish is
confined they will set it free. The wind will do the rest. Scattering the
rubbish all over the city. Paper, tins, old rags and of course the wonderful
smell of rotting vegetables. Soon every park, every garden will be reduced
to ... Utter Garbage! (*He laughs at his cunning*)
Hamilton You'll never get away with it.
Vermin Oh, but we will. Especially when they (*the audience*) get tired of
  trying to keep it tidy. And they will. So what d'you say, Binlid?
Binlid Well ... (*playing for time*) I'd like to think it over first if that's all right
  with you, Your Ratship.

Vermin Of course, of course. But don't think too much will you? You know
my views on thinking. Ten minutes should be long enough, I'll come back
for your answer then. Let's hope it's the right one.

Binlid realizes the threat in Vermin's tone and gulps audibly

Ten minutes then. (*Still unsure of Hamilton*) And maybe your cousin will
tell us more of the story of her tail.
Trash Oh very funny Your Ratship; story tail, tail story …

Trash doubles over with laughter, facing the audience

Vermin Well I'm so glad I amuse you, Mr Trash. Now if the guards will lend
me a spear for a moment I'll allow you to return the compliment and amuse
me for a while.

*A Guard hands his spear to Vermin who prods Trash in the rump. Trash
responds in the usual manner of a small creature poked in a tender place with
a sharp object*

Ten minutes.

Vermin prods Trash again and they and the Guards leave

Hamilton What a dirty, rotten rat. And he tried to threaten you, you know
that.
Binlid 'E's not a rat to be trifled with, the Lord Vermin.
Hamilton You're never going to give in to him?
Binlid Don't see as there's much else I can do. He's the Ruler of the Refuse.
He's the …
Hamilton Guardian of the Garbage, yes I know, I heard him. Look why don't
you just leave?
Binlid Leave? (*This is a new and horrifying concept to him*)
Hamilton Yes.
Binlid Leave the dump?
Hamilton Yes. Oh, come on, come with me. We'll look for this better world
that Dumpster saw from the roof. It must be out there somewhere all we
have to do is find it.
Binlid I can't do that. I can't leave the dump.
Hamilton Why ever not?
Binlid Well, 'e won't like it for a start.
Hamilton He's got nothing to do with it. You're a free animal. You can go

where you want. He might be the Lord Vermin but he doesn't own you. It's against a rodent's rights, so it is.

Binlid 'E is very possessive of 'is subjects. And 'e's got a nasty temper when he's crossed. 'E'd bite your ears off. 'E would, no messin' I've seen 'im do it.

Hamilton Guardian of the Garbage? Huh! More like Gaoler of the Junk heap. Warden of the Waste-tip. You're a prisoner here, Mr Binlid. As much in a cage as I used to be. At least there were steel bars to keep me in. You've only got your own fear of Vermin keeping you in this dump. (*She throws down her sling and bandages and makes to leave*) Well he doesn't frighten me. I'm leaving. If I stay in this place it'll mean poor old Dumpster died for nothing. Good-day.

The reference to Dumpster's apparent death stirs something in Binlid

Binlid Well, anyway ... What if I did leave? The dump I mean. Where would I go? I don't know any place else. Lived 'ere all my life. What would I eat? Where would I sleep? (*Having second thoughts*) I don't know ...

Hamilton Mr Binlid, are you are a man or a mouse?

Binlid I'm a rat.

Hamilton Then act like one. Look, there must have been time when rats didn't live in garbage. When they lived in hedges and forests and ate berries and fresh food, not potato peelings and chicken bones. A time when they were free animals and not ruled by the likes of Vermin and his plan to turn the world into a rubbish dump.

Binlid considers this for a while

Binlid An' you think that's what Dumpster wanted?

Hamilton I'm sure of it. And not only for himself.

Binlid 'E'll come after us, you know. Vermin. 'E won't let us get away. An' when 'e catches us ...

Hamilton Then we'll have to catch him first. What we need is a cunning plan.

Binlid What we need is a cat.

Music: the theme from Captain Pugwash

Captain Rodent (*off*) Starboard a little and steady as she goes, Mr Bilge. I think I see a light up ahead ...

The sardine can with Captain Rodent, Bilge and propelled by the Sea-Rats emerges from the grid and travels across the front of the garbage. Their attention is on the audience. In the can is the life-belt and Binlid's broken alarm clock with its face hanging on the end of the main spring and tied to a thick rope

I think we've been here before, Mr Bilge. Really must get this port and starboard business sorted out. Right. Well, prepare to run aground then.
Hamilton (*to Binlid*) Come on, I've seen him do this before.

Hamilton and Binlid take cover behind the garbage. The sardine can beaches as before tipping on to its side and spilling the crew, the clock and the life-belt into a heap on the floor. Sound effects of a ship running aground

Captain Rodent Another successful land fall for Captain Rodent and his band of intrepid mariners.

Binlid recognizes his former possessions

Binlid 'Ere that's my bed. What are you lot doin' in my bed? And that's my alarm clock. Where'd you find my alarm clock? Come on give it back.

The Sea-Rats hold Binlid off from Captain Rodent

Bilge I'm afraid this alarm clock is material evidence to the sinking of the Good Ship *Wastage*, and as such is the property of a court martial. We fished it out of the gutter where the ship sank.
Binlid Well it belongs to me. I 'ad it this morning only it wouldn't stop ringing see, so I threw it up in the air ... I just didn't see where it landed that's all.
Captain Rodent It landed on my ship. Went straight through the bottom of the jolly old box. Lucky we weren't all drowned.
Binlid Oh. I'm sorry. I didn't realize ...
Captain Rodent I say, aren't you that Hamster chap from the other side of the sewer?
Hamilton I am. Look, I'm sorry about ——
Captain Rodent Where's the young chap, the one with the dream. Er ... Dumpster, yes I think that was his name.
Binlid Dumpster? 'E's my nephew, or rather was.
Hamilton There was a bit of an accident and I'm afraid Dumpster was ... I'm afraid he's ...
Binlid What she's tryin' to say is 'e was run over by lorry while chasin' after 'is dream.
Captain Rodent Gosh. What rotten luck. I think this calls for caps off, Mr Bilge.

Bilge Ship's company, off caps. Mark of respect for a Sea-Rat no longer with us.

The Sea-Rats stand to attention and remove their caps, as do Bilge and Captain Rodent. The Last Post sounds quietly under the following exchanges

Deepest condolences, sir. We didn't know him for long but we sort of took to the little rat.

Capt Rodent Yes. Terrifically sorry. Sort of feel a bit to blame: giving him a lift in the boat and all that.

Binlid It's not your fault. It was always on the cards.

Capt Rodent Even so if there's anything we can do …

Binlid No. Thanks anyway, but I'm all right. Really.

Capt Rodent Maybe a bit of a memorial to the little chap?

Hamilton Actually, there is something you could do. You could help us make a bit of Dumpster's dream come true.

Capt Rodent Yes. Delighted, if we can. Mr Bilge?

Bilge and the Sea-Rats nod their approval enthusiastically

Hamilton Good. We need to really frighten the rat who rules this dump, the Lord Vermin …

The Sea-Rats show they know about Vermin if only by reputation

Captain Rodent The Lord Vermin.

Hamilton We've got to get him so scared that he *will* let us go and search for Dumpster's better world, and he *won't* chase after us. Ever.

Captain Rodent Well, he's a difficult man to scare, the Lord Vermin. What you need is a cunning plan.

Bilge What you need is a cat.

Binlid Yeah. I think we got this far by ourselves.

Bilge It doesn't have to be a real cat. It just has to be real enough to convince Vermin it's a cat. It's just a question of supplying the right combination of audiovisual stimuli.

Captain Rodent Well stitch another leg on my trousers and call me a lobster if Mr Bilge isn't the brightest First Mate afloat.

Bilge I don't think a lobster has ——

Captain Rodent Right, let's get to it. You men: into the garbage see what you can find to make one of these cat stimuli things.

Captain Rodent supervises as Binlid and the Sea-Rats dig around in the

*garbage and find pieces of rubbish to make the "cat". They show each other
the pieces they have found in full view of the audience. When all the
component parts have been so displayed they carry them around the back of
the heap of rubbish and assemble them, maybe with the help of hidden stage
assistants. The audience are not shown the assembled "cat". While they are
doing this, Bilge and Hamilton move* DS *to the audience*

Hamilton Have you met the child-people?
Bilge Once or twice.
Hamilton Vermin's as frightened of them as he is of cats. Do you think they
could help us out?
Bilge Well we need someone to make the noise of a cat and none of us have
got very loud voices. I don't think we can do it without their help.
Hamilton Will you do it, will you help us?

The audience should respond positively

Will you make the noise of a cat when I tell you to?

The audience respond again

I knew I could depend on you. Right, this is what I want you to do ...

*Hamilton organizes the audience to miaow in unison on a given signal and
rehearses them a couple of times with the help of Bilge*

Magic! Now don't forget. Wait till I give the signal.

Trash blows his fanfare, off

He's here, we'd better hide. (*To the audience*) Now don't forget. Oops,
better hide the boat. Be a bit of a give-away if he sees this here.

*Hamilton and Bilge drag the sardine can and the clock around the back of
the rubbish heap but forget to pick up the life-belt. They take their places in
the garbage; Bilge to operate the "cat" with the others, and Hamilton to lead
the audience, to whom she must be clearly visible while giving the impression
of hiding*

Vermin, Trash and the two Guards enter

Vermin (*looking at his watch*) Ten minutes and thirty-two seconds. So,

Binlid, what's it going to be? (*He walks suspiciously around the empty dump*) Binlid?

Trash He's very quiet, Your Ratship.

Vermin Too quiet ... (*He finds the life-belt*) I smell a rat.

Hamilton gives the signal. The "cat" is displayed and animated by Binlid and the others. Hamilton leads the shouts of miaow from the audience. There are hisses, spits and supporting cat noises

Trash is completely terror-struck and cowers on the floor toward the audience covering his head and shouting

Trash Aah, it's a cat, it's a cat ... Don't eat me, don't eat me. I don't want to die.

The Guards take up uneasy defensive positions near him. Vermin is initially taken by surprise but soon recovers. He beckons the Guards and they pull aside some of the rubbish to reveal Binlid and the others operating the "cat". As they realize their plan is foiled they one by one give up their part in the "cat". The last to realize the game is up is Hamilton who is leading the miaow from the audience, which gradually peters out

Hamilton Miaow! Miaow! Miaow ... miaow?

The Guards hold Binlid and the others at spear point. Vermin's attention turns to Trash who is still on the floor and terrified

Trash Don't eat me, don't eat me. I don't want to die! I don't want to die! Aah, aah ... (*and so on ad lib*)

Vermin walks up to Trash and pushes him over with his foot

No no no no no ... (*Realization dawns*) Oh, Lord Vermin.

Vermin Get up. (*Turning his attention back to Binlid and the others*) Ingenious. A cunning plan indeed. Unfortunately for you I do not scare as easily as my valet here. So this is how you repay me, Binlid. After all I've done for you.

Binlid You've never done nothin' for me 'cept keep me 'ere in this stinkin' dump.

Hamilton You tell him.

Vermin You realize this is treason. And there is only one punishment for treason.

Captain Rodent You wouldn't talk so big if there weren't more of you than there are of us, you coward.

A quick glance around and he has second thoughts about this statement. Bilge just shakes his head in despair at his CO

Vermin Captain Rodent, I believe. The most unsuccessful sailor since Christopher Columbus nipped out to the Indian takeaway and discovered Kentucky Fried Chicken.

Captain Rodent Really, I must protest ...

Vermin But it's of no consequence now. (*He is standing in front of the drain spout*) So, before we say goodbye. Have you any last requests? Any futile pleas for mercy? Any anguished cries of remorse?

Vermin signals the Guards and they raise their spears

There is sound of Dumpster screaming as he shoots down the drain

Dumpster (*off*) Ahhhhh!

Dumpster hurtles out of the drain spout and lands on Vermin

Hamilton Dumpster!
Binlid Well stone me.

The Guards and Trash are completely dumbstruck. Bilge seizes his chance and leads the Sea-Rats as they overpower the Guards

The Guards are chased off

Trash does not escape and is held by the Sea-Rats. Vermin is helpless under Dumpster

Binlid Great rats'-tails, Dumpster, we thought you was dead.
Dumpster So did I. Hallo, Hamilton.
Hamilton Hallo, Dumpster.
Dumpster Hallo, Lord Vermin. What're doing down there?
Vermin (*speechless with rage*) Grrr ...

Captain Rodent and Binlid help Dumpster to his feet and take hold of Vermin. He is brought DS to join Trash and the Sea-Rats

Captain Rodent Good job you turned up when you did, young fella. Things were looking a bit tricky there for a minute.

Binlid Yeah, not 'arf. How d'you get on the roof?

Dumpster Not sure. I remember holding on to Hamilton as these huge headlights came towards us, and then a funny feeling like flying through the air. And then I woke up on the roof. I'm afraid I fell down the drain pipe again.

Binlid Lucky you did. Vermin was about to do us all in.

Hamilton He was going to turn the whole world into a huge rubbish dump. But I think you've put a stop to that.

Dumpster Not me. The child-people. That's why Vermin's so scared of them, isn't it? *(To Vermin)* I did some thinking on the roof and I worked it all out. You see they can count. And because they can count they can do sums. And when they do sums they find that all this rubbish doesn't add up. Because one day, if they're not careful, there'll be more rubbish than places for people to live.

Hamilton Yes, I suppose so, but I don't see what can they do about it ...

Dumpster Well some of the rubbish can be used again. All the glass and tins and paper can be collected up and ... and ...

Bilge Recycled. I think it's called recycling.

Vermin Rubbish! They'll never do it. People never do. They don't care until it's too late.

Dumpster Child-people do, and you know it. If they can ... recycle only half the rubbish then there'll be ...

Binlid Only half as much.

Hamilton And only half as many dumps.

Captain Rodent And twice as many nice places left to live in.

Bilge *(impressed with his CO)* Oh, well done, sir. Well done.

Vermin *(contemptuously)* Counting!

Dumpster Yes. We're going to learn to count.

Hamilton And you don't count! Not any more.

Binlid So what are we going to do with him?

Captain Rodent I think you can leave that to me. I know where there's a court martial just waiting to happen. I'm sure they'd be really pleased to meet the rascal who tried to harpoon a sea captain and his crew of jolly sea-rats. What d'you think, Mr Bilge?

Bilge I'll get the ship ready, sir.

Bilge and the Sea-Rats assemble the sardine can and escort Vermin and Trash aboard

Captain Rodent Well, better be getting along. Time and tide and all that.

Speaking of which, I'd like to keep the alarm clock if I may. Evidence, you know. Could save my tail.

Binlid Yeah, least I can do under the circumstances.

Captain Rodent Good luck, young rat. We can give you a lift if you want to carry on looking for your better world.

Dumpster No thanks. I've found my world. It's right here. It just needs tidying up a bit, that's all.

Bilge Beg pardon, sir. Prisoners all aboard. Ready to cast off.

Captain Rodent Very good, Mr Bilge.

He salutes Dumpster and boards the sardine can

And if you see us sailing past again, you might give us a wave?

Trash Oh, yes. Sailing waves. Waves sailing. Very funny.

Vermin Do shut up, Trash.

The sardine can with Captain Rodent, Vermin and Trash propelled by the Sea-Rats moves through the grid opened by Bilge, and leaves

Binlid It's good to 'ave you back, Dumpster. But I think we've got some work to do before you can say you're glad to be back. Come on, the sooner we start the sooner we finish.

Dumpster How about if we collect all the newspapers into one pile, all the tins and cans into another and all the bottles into another?

Hamilton That sounds like a good idea. Come on.

They all set about tidying the rubbish. Several bundles of newspapers, a number of black plastic sacks full of tins and a couple of cardboard boxes full of bottles are produced from the rubbish heap. Three neat piles of sorted refuse are quickly formed

Dumpster Look! Uncle Binlid, Hamilton look at this.

Binlid Well stone me.

Hamilton It looks like a ...

In the centre of the rubbish is a small brightly coloured flower

Dumpster It is. It's a flower. A real flower.

Binlid 'Ow did that get here?

Dumpster It must have been here all the time. But we couldn't see it for the rubbish.

Dumpster carefully scoops up the flower and brings it DS *where he replants it, crouching down to look at it. Binlid and Hamilton follow*

The first flower of a better world.
Binlid You know, I think this dream of yours might come true after all.
Hamilton Well. I think that's up to us, isn't it?

The Lights dim leaving a single spot on the flower. All withdraw. Music

They all return to sing the song "Utter Garbage" (see page 35) with the audience:

Song: Utter Garbage

All   Collect all your rubbish,
                          Your papers and glass,
                          Sift it and sort it,
                          Make room, see the grass.

                          When you go camping,
                          Or out for a trip,
                          Don't leave the place
                          Like a big rubbish tip.

                          There's things we can use
                          In what gets thrown away,
                          Let's sift it and sort it
                          Starting today.

Black-out

CURTAIN

Utter Garbage

Music by Nigel Bennetts
Lyrics by Jane Thompson

FURNITURE AND PROPERTY LIST

ACT I

On stage: Rubbish (newspapers, black plastic sacks containing tins, cardboard
boxes filled with bottles, etc.)
Sardine can
Alarm clock
Plate
Morsels of food
Aerosol air-freshener
Brush
Blanket for sardine can ship
Sticks for sardine can ship
Flowers (Garden scene)

Off stage: Horn (**Trash**)
Spears (**Guards**)
Megaphone (**Captain Rodent**)
Small trolley with life-belt. *On it:* telescope (**Sea-Rats**)

ACT II

Set: All "rubbish" props to make the "cat"
White strips of cloth for bandage
Soft drink can with water for first-aid
Flower

Off stage: Takeaway bag containing hamburger (**Binlid**)
Sardine can ship. *On it:* life-belt, Binlid's broken alarm clock, rope
(**Sea-Rats**)
Spears (**Guards**)

LIGHTING PLOT

ACT I

To open: Full stage lighting on rubbish dump; dull and dirty

Cue 1   **Captain Rodent** and his crew pass into the garden   (Page 14)
    Change lighting to reflect brighter, cleaner scene

Cue 2   Music: the theme from *The Great Escape*   (Page 19)
    Car headlight effect sweeps throughout auditorium

Cue 3   **Dumpster** and **Hamilton** collide on the stage   (Page 20)
    Snap headlight sweeping effect, catch **Dumpster** *and*
    Hamilton *in strong spotlight*

Cue 4   Huge crash   (Page 20)
    Black-out

ACT II

To open: Rubbish dump lighting

Cue 5   **Hamilton**: " ... that's up to us, isn't it?"   (Page 34)
    Lights dim to a single spot on the flower

Cue 6   The **Company** enter for the song   (Page 34)
    Bring up full lighting

Cue 7   When ready after song finishes   (Page 34)
    Black-out

EFFECTS PLOT

ACT I

Cue 1	At opening	(Page 1)
	Music; fade when ready	
Cue 2	When ready	(Page 1)
	Alarm clock	
Cue 3	**Binlid** hurls alarm clock off	(Page 1)
	Snap off alarm; breaking clock and release of mainspring	
Cue 4	**Dumpster** disappears up the drain spout	(Page 9)
	Captain Pugwash *music for* **Captain Rodent**'s *entrance*	